SELF-IMPROVEMENT THROUGH PUBLIC SPEAKING

Dr. Orison Swett Marden

Executive Books

Laws of Leadership Series, Volume II

SELF-IMPROVEMENT THROUGH PUBLIC SPEAKING
Orison Swett Marden

Published by
Executive Books
206 West Allen Street
Mechanicsburg, PA 17055
717-766-9499   800-233-2665
Fax: 717-766-6565
www.ExecutiveBooks.com

ISBN-13: 978-1-933715-27-8
ISBN-10: 1-933715-27-8

Cover Design and Interior Layout
by Gregory Dixon

Printed in the United States of America

Table of Contents

Introduction. 5

The Wisdom of Orison Swett Marden 9

Self-Improvement Through Public Speaking. . . 13

If You Can Talk Well 37

Recommended Reading 61

Introduction

*S*elf-Improvement Through Public Speaking, by medical doctor and attorney Orison Swett Marden, is especially important. For over a hundred years this volume became known as "...the magic book about public speaking!"

Orison Swett Marden observed, "The Creator has not given you a longing to do that which you have no ability to do." He knew, just as research has confirmed again and again, that public speaking is essential to your success. Your ability to effectively communicate is vital, if you are addressing one person, three radio microphones, a press conference, or a vast audience composed mostly of people you do not know.

If you are like most people, public speaking is most likely not your favorite pastime. Experience shows us all that platform presentation skills are crucial to success in your work place. This ability is not only needed for your career, but in your personal and social life as well.

The person with strong verbal communication skills has a clear advantage over almost all others who remain reluctant, afraid, bashful, tongue-tied, uncertain about speaking, or unwilling to try speaking. The skilled speaker has many advantages even over the more senior colleagues who have not developed their speaking skills.

Marden became a successful speaker by overcoming his stage fright while a young man. Next he overcame all obstacles that limited or prevented his ability to become a polished speaker.

Orison Swett Marden (1850-1924), the founder of *Success Magazine*, is also considered the founder of the present "self-help" or "personal success" movement in America. He has developed insights that have influenced best-selling authors and lecturers from past and present such as Napoleon Hill, Dale Carnegie, Og Mandino, Norman Vincent Peale, Steven Covey, Don Hutson, Danny Cox, Jeffrey Gitomer, Brian Tracy, and many others.

Orison Swett Marden was born in a poor family on a New England farm in 1850. Marden graduated from Boston University in 1871 and also attended Andover Theological Seminary and Harvard. He received his M.D. at Harvard in 1881 and also obtained an LL.B. degree from Harvard in 1882. In addition, Marden studied at the Boston School of Oratory before embarking upon various ventures in resort development and hotel ownership.

After a series of business successes and setbacks, Marden went to Boston in the 1890s to receive a fresh start. It was during this season in his life that he was influenced profoundly by a book he found in an attic. Marden admitted that after reading English writer Samuel Smiles' book entitled *Self-Help*, he set a goal for himself to become the Samuel Smiles of America. Marden once wrote, "The little book was the friction which wakened the spark sleeping in the flint." He later drew inspiration from other prolific writers such as Oliver Wendell Holmes and Emerson, but Samuel Smiles, his greatest hero, shaped his career and inspired much of his writings.

The central theme of his books was optimism. His first book, published in 1894, *Pushing to the Front*, was distributed with tremendous success. Marden also achieved enormous success when he founded *Success Magazine* in 1897 which reached a circulation of approximately half-million with an estimated readership of two to three million. *Success Magazine* was discontinued in 1912 due to financial challenges, and in 1918, Marden started a new version of *Success* that was achieving rapid growth until his death in 1924.

From the time he started writing, Orison Swett Marden averaged about two books per year, and became one of the most influential figures of his day. His books include *The Miracle of Right Thought, Self-Investment, He Can Who Thinks He Can, Thoughts About Character, Success Nuggets, Exceptional Employee, Choosing A Career, Keeping Fit, Friendship, Crime of Silence, How to Get What You Want, Masterful Personality, Not The Salary But The Opportunity,* and many others.

Forrest Wallace Cato

The Wisdom of Orison Swett Marden

A strong, successful man is not the victim of his environment. He creates favorable conditions.

All who have accomplished great things have had a great aim, have fixed their gaze on a goal which was high, one which sometimes seemed impossible.

Deep within man dwells those slumbering powers; powers that would astonish him, that he never dreamed of possessing; forces that would revolutionize his life if aroused and put into action.

Many a man has finally succeeded only because he has failed after repeated efforts. If he had never met defeat he would never have known any great victory.

Every youth owes it to himself and to the world to make the most possible out of the stuff that is in him.

Joyfulness keeps the heart and face young. A good laugh makes us better friends with ourselves and everybody around us.

Most of our obstacles would melt away if, instead of cowering before them, we should make up our minds to walk boldly through them.

Nothing else so destroys the power to stand alone as the habit of leaning upon others. If you lean, you will never be strong or original. Stand alone or bury your ambition to be somebody in the world.

Our thoughts and imagination are the only real limits to our possibilities.

The best thing about giving of ourselves is that what we get is always better than what we give. The reaction is greater than the action.

Success is not measured by what you accomplish, but by the opposition you have encountered, and the courage with which you have maintained the struggle against overwhelming odds.

The golden opportunity you are seeking is in yourself. It is not in your environment; it is not in luck or chance, or the help of others; it is in yourself alone.

There can be no great courage where there is no confidence or assurance, and half the battle is in the conviction that we can do what we undertake.

There is only one thing for us to do, and that is to do our level best right where we are every day of our lives; To use our best judgment, and then to trust the rest to that Power which holds the forces of the universe in his hands.

Wisdom is knowledge which has become a part of one's being.

You cannot measure a man by his failures. You must know what use he makes of them. What did they mean to him. What did he get out of them.

It does not matter how strong most of our mental faculties are, if they are not led by a vigorous faith. Faith puts all the other faculties to work. Its influence upon the mental faculties is very bracing, while that of doubt and fear is demoralizing, deteriorating. There is nothing that will so brace man up, will so buttress and reinforce his weaker faculties, as a robust self-faith, faith in himself, faith in everybody and in everything, faith that there is a great, magnificent force in civilization, in the affairs of man, a current which runs Godward; that there is a divinely beneficent purpose running through the universe.

Self-Improvement Through Public Speaking

By Dr. Orison Swett Marden

It does not matter whether he wants to be a public speaker or not, a person should have such complete control of himself, should be so self-reliant and self-poised, that he can get up in any audience, no matter how large or formidable, and express his thoughts clearly and distinctly.

> **"Self-expression in some manner is the only means of developing mental power."**

Self-expression in some manner is the only means of developing mental power. It may be in music; it may be on canvas; it may be through public speaking; it may come through selling goods or writing a book; but it must come through self-expression.

13

Self-expression in any legitimate form tends to call out what is in a man, his resourcefulness, inventiveness; but no other form of self-expression develops a man so thoroughly and so effectively, and so quickly unfolds all of his powers, as speaking before an audience.

It is doubtful whether anyone can reach the highest standard of culture without studying the art of expression, especially public vocal expression. In all ages public speaking has been regarded as the highest expression of human achievement. Young people, no matter what they intend to be, whether blacksmith or farmer, merchant or physician, should make it a study.

Nothing else will call out what is in a man so quickly and so effectively as the constant effort to do his best in speaking before an audience. When one undertakes to think on his feet and speak extemporaneously before the public, the power and the skill of the entire man are put to a severe test.

The practice of public speaking, the effort to marshal all one's forces in a logical and forceful manner, to bring to a focus all the power one possesses, is a great awakener of all the faculties. The sense of power that comes from holding the attention, stirring the emotions, or convincing the reason of an audience, gives self-confidence, assurance, self-reliance, arouses ambition and tends to make one more effective in every way.

One's judgment, education, manhood, character, all the things that go to make a man what he is, are being unrolled like a panorama in his effort to express himself. Every mental faculty is quickened, every power of thought and expression stirred and spurred. The speaker summons all his reserves of experience, of

> **One's judgment, education, manhood, character, all the things that go to make a man what he is, are being unrolled like a panorama in his effort to express himself.**

knowledge, of natural or acquired ability, and masses all his forces in the endeavor to express himself with power and to capture the approval and applause of his audience.

Such an effort takes hold of the entire nature, beads the brow, fires the eye. flushes the cheek, and sends the blood surging through the veins. Dormant impulses are stirred, half-forgotten memories revived, the imagination quickened to see figures and similes that would never come to calm thought.

This forced awakening of the whole personality has effects reaching much further than the oratorical occasion. The effort to marshal all one's reserves in a logical and orderly manner, to bring to the front all the power one possesses, leaves these reserves permanently better in hand, more readily in reach.

A writer has the advantage of being able to wait for his moods. He can write when he feels like it; and he knows that he can burn his manuscript again and again if it does not suit him. There are not a thousand eyes upon him. He does not have a great audience criticizing every sentence, weighing every thought. He does not have to step upon the scales of every listener's judgment to be weighed, as does the public speaker. He may write as listlessly as he pleases, use much or little of his brain or energy, just as he chooses or feels like doing. No one is watching him. His pride and vanity are not touched, and what he writes may never be seen by anyone. Then, there is always a chance for revision. In music, whether vocal or instrumental, what one gives out is only partially one's own; the rest is the composer's. In conversation, we do not feel that so much depends upon our words; only a few persons hear them, and perhaps no one will ever think of them again. But when a person attempts to speak before an audience, all props are knocked out from under him; he has nothing to lean upon, he can get no assistance, no advice: he must find all his resources in himself; he stands absolutely alone. He may

> **"Anyone who lays any claim to culture should train himself to think on his feet, so that he can at a moment's notice rise and express himself intelligently."**

have millions of money, broad acres of land, and may live in a palace, but none of these avail him now; his memory, his experience, his education, his ability, are all he has; he must be measured by what he says, what he reveals of himself in his speech; he must stand or fall in the estimation of his audience.

Anyone who lays any claim to culture should train himself to think on his feet, so that he can at a moment's notice rise and express himself intelligently. The occasions for after-dinner speaking are increasing enormously. A great many questions which once were settled in the office are now discussed and disposed of at dinners. All sorts of business deals are now carried through at dinners. There was never before any such demand for dinner public speaking as today.

We know men who have, by dint of hard work and persistent grit, lifted themselves into positions of prominence, and yet they are not able to stand on their feet in public, even to make a few remarks or to put a motion, without trembling like an aspen leaf. They had plenty of opportunities when they were young, at school, in debating clubs, to get rid of their self-consciousness and to acquire ease and facility in public speaking, but they always shrank from every opportunity, because they were timid, or felt that somebody else could handle the debate or questions better.

There are plenty of business men today who would give a great deal of money if they could only go back and improve the early opportunities for learning to think and speak on their feet which they threw away. Now they have money, they have position, but they are nobodies when called upon to speak in public. All they can do is to look foolish, blush, stammer out an apology, and sit down.

Some time ago I was at a public meeting when a man who stands very high in the community, who is king in his specialty, was called upon to give his opinion upon the matter under consideration, and he got up and trembled and

> **"Probably he would have given anything if he had early in life trained himself to speak extemporaneously, so that he could think on his feet and say with power and effectiveness that which he knew."**

stammered and could scarcely say his soul was his own. He could not even make a decent appearance. He had power and a great deal of experience, but there he stood, as helpless as a child, and he felt cheap, mortified, embarrassed. Probably he would have given anything if he had early in life trained himself to speak extemporaneously, so that he could think on his feet and say with power and effectiveness that which he knew.

At the very meeting where this strong man, who had the respect and confidence of everybody who knew him, had made such a miserable failure of his attempt to give his opinion upon the important public matter on which he was well posted, a shallow-brained business man of the same city who hadn't a hundredth part of the other man's practical power in affair, got up and made a brilliant speech, and strangers no doubt thought that he was much the stronger man. He had simply cultivated the ability to say his best thing on his feet, and the other man had not.

A brilliant young man in New York, who has climbed to a responsible position in a very short time, tells me that he has been surprised on several occasions when he has been called upon to speak at banquets, or at other public functions, at the new discoveries he has made of himself of power which he never before dreamed he possessed, and he now regrets more than anything else that he has in the past allowed so many opportunities for calling himself out to go by.

The effort to express one's ideas in lucid, clean-cut, concise, telling English tends to make one's everyday language choicer and more direct, and to improve one's diction generally. In this and other ways speech-making develops mental power and character. This explains the rapidity with which a young man develops in school or college when he begins to take part in public debates or in debating societies.

"In thinking on one's feet before an audience, one must think quickly, vigorously, effectively. At the same time he must speak through a properly modulated voice, with proper facial and bodily expression and gesture. This requires practice in early life."

Every man, says Lord Chesterfield, may choose good words instead of bad ones and speak properly instead of improperly; he may have grace in his motions and gestures, and may be a very agreeable instead of disagreeable speaker if he will take care and pains.

It is a matter of painstaking and preparation. There is everything in learning what you wish to know. Your vocal culture, manner, and mental furnishing, are to be made a matter for thought and careful training.

In thinking on one's feet before an audience, one must think quickly, vigorously, effectively. At the same time he must speak through a properly modulated voice, with proper facial and bodily expression and gesture. This requires practice in early life.

Nothing will tire an audience more quickly than monotony, everything expressed on the

> **"Gladstone said: 'Ninety-nine men in every hundred never rise above mediocrity because the training of the voice is entirely neglected and considered of no importance.'"**

same dead level. There must be variety; the human mind tires very quickly when this is not supplied.

This is especially true of a monotonous tone. It is a great art to be able to raise and lower the voice with sweet flowing cadences which please the ear.

Gladstone said: "Ninety-nine men in every

hundred never rise above mediocrity because the training of the voice is entirely neglected and considered of no importance."

An early training for effective speaking will make one careful to secure a good vocabulary by good reading and a dictionary. One must know words.

Close, compact statement is imperative. Learn to stop when you get through. Do not keep stringing out conversation or argument after you have made your point. You only neutralize the good impression you have made, weaken your case, and prejudice people against you for your lack of tact, good judgment, or sense of proportion.

The Debating Club is the nursery of public speakers. No matter how far you have to go to attend it, or how much trouble it is, or how difficult it is to get the time, the drill you will get by it is often the turning point. Lincoln, Wilson, Webster, Choate, Clay, and Patrick Henry got their training in the old-fashioned Debating Society.

Do not think that because you do not know anything about parliamentary law you should not accept the presidency of your club or debating society, or take an active part. This is just the place to learn, and when you have accepted the position you can post yourself on the rules, and the chances are that you will never know the rules until you are thrust into the chair where you will be obliged to give rulings. Join just as many young people's organizations—especially self-improvement organizations—as you can, and force yourself to speak every time you get a chance. If the

> **"Every time you rise to your feet will increase your confidence, and after a while you will form the habit of speaking until it will be as easy as anything else."**

chance does not come to you, make it. Jump to your feet and say something upon every question that is up for discussion. Do not be afraid to rise to put a motion or to second it or to give your opinion upon it. Do not wait until you are better prepared. You never will be.

Every time you rise to your feet will increase your confidence, and after a while you will form the habit of speaking until it will be as easy as anything else. There is no one thing which will develop young people so rapidly and effectively as debating clubs and discussions of all sorts. A vast number of our public men have owed their advance more to the old-fashioned debating societies than anything else. Here they learned confidence, self-reliance; they discovered themselves. It was here they learned not to be afraid of themselves, to express their opinions with force and independence. Nothing will call a young man out more than the struggle to hold his own in a debate. It is strong, vigorous exercise for the mind just as wrestling is for the body.

Do not remain way back on the rear seat. Go up front. Do not be afraid to show yourself. This shrinking into a corner and getting out of sight and avoiding publicity is fatal to self-confidence.

It is so easy and tempting, especially for boys and girls in school or college, to shrink from the public debates or speaking, on the ground that they are not quite well enough educated at present. They want to wait until they can use a little better grammar, until they have read more history and more literature, until they have gained a little more culture and ease of manner.

But the way to acquire grace, ease, facility, the way to get poise and balance so that you will not feel disturbed in public gatherings, is to get the experience. Do the thing so many times that it will become second nature to you. If you have an invitation to speak, no matter how much you may shrink from it, or how timid or shy you may be, resolve that you will not let this opportunity for self-enlargement slip by you.

> "If you have an invitation to speak, no matter how much you may shrink from it, or how timid or shy you may be, resolve that you will not let this opportunity for self-enlargement slip by you."

I know of a young man who has a great deal of natural ability for public speaking, and yet he is so timid that he always shrinks from accepting invitations to speak at banquets or in public because he is so afraid that he has not had experience enough. He lacks confidence in himself. He is so proud, and so afraid that he will make some slip which will mortify him, that he has waited and waited and waited until now he is discouraged and thinks that he will never be able to do anything in public speaking at all. He would give anything in the world if he had only accepted all of the invitations he has had, because then he would have profited by experience. It would have been a thousand times better for him to have made a mistake, or even to have broken down entirely a few times, than to have missed the scores of opportunities which would undoubtedly have made a strong public speaker of him.

"What is technically called 'stage fright' is very common."

What is technically called "stage fright" is very common. A college boy recited an address "To the conscript fathers." His professor asked,—"Is that the way Caesar would have spoken it?" "Yes," he replied, "if Caesar had been scared half to death, and as nervous as a cat."

An almost fatal timidity seizes on an inexperienced person when he knows that all eyes are watching him, that everybody in his audience is trying to measure and weigh him, studying him, scrutinizing him to see how much there is in him, for what he stands, and making up their minds whether he measures more or less than they expected.

Some men are constitutionally sensitive and so afraid of being gazed at that they don't dare open their mouths, even when a question in which they are deeply interested and on which they have strong views is being dis-

> **"But no public speaker can make a great impression until he gets rid of himself, until he can absolutely annihilate his self-consciousness, forget himself in his speech."**

cussed. At debating clubs, meetings of literary societies, or gatherings of any kind. they sit dumb, longing, yet fearing to speak. The sound of their own voices, if they should get on their feet to make a motion or to speak in a public gathering, would paralyze them. The mere thought of asserting themselves, of putting forward their views or opinions on any subject as being worthy of attention, or as valuable as those of their companions, makes them blush and shrink more into themselves.

This timidity is often, however, not so much the fear of one's audience, as the fear lest one can make no suitable expression of his thought.

The hardest thing for the public speaker to overcome is self-consciousness. Those terrible eyes which pierce him through and through, which are measuring him, criticizing him, are very difficult to get out of his consciousness.

But no public speaker can make a great impression until he gets rid of himself, until he can absolutely annihilate his self-consciousness, forget himself in his speech. While he is wondering what kind of an impression he is making, what people think of him, his power is crippled, and his speech to that extent will be mechanical, wooden.

Even a partial failure on the platform has good results, for it often arouses a determination to conquer the next time, which never leaves one. Demosthenes' heroic efforts, and Disraeli's "The time will come when you will hear me," are historic examples.

It is not the speech, but the man behind the speech, that wins a way to the front.

One man carries weight because he is himself the embodiment of power, he is himself convinced of what he says. There is nothing of the negative, the doubtful, the uncertain in his nature. He not only knows a thing, but he knows that he knows it. His opinion carries with it the entire weight of his being. The whole man gives consent to his judgment. He himself is in his conviction, in his act.

"It is not the speech, but the man behind the speech, that wins a way to the front."

One of the most entrancing speakers I have ever listened to—a man to hear whom people would go long distances and stand for hours to get admission to the hall where he spoke— never was able to get the confidence of his audience because he lacked character. People liked to be swayed by his eloquence. There was a great charm in the cadences of his perfect sentences. But somehow they could not believe what he said.

The public speaker must be sincere. The public is very quick to see through shams. If the audience sees mud at the bottom of your eye, that you are not honest yourself, that you are acting, they will not take any stock in you.

It is not enough to say a pleasing thing, an interesting thing, the public speaker must be able to convince; and to convince others he must himself have strong convictions.

Very few people ever rise to their greatest possibilities or ever know their entire

> **"It would be difficult to estimate the great part which practical drill in public speaking may play in one's life."**

power unless confronted by some great occasion. We are as much amazed as others are when, in some great emergency we outdo ourselves. Somehow the power that stands behind us in the silence, in the depths of our natures comes to our relief, intensifies our faculties a thousandfold and enables us to do things which before we thought impossible.

It would be difficult to estimate the great

part which practical drill in public speaking may play in one's life.

Great occasions, when nations have been in peril, have developed and brought out some of the greatest public speakers of the world. Cicero, Mirabeau, Patrick Henry, Webster, and John Bright might all be called to witness to this fact.

The occasion had much to do with the greatest speech delivered in the United States Senate—Webster's reply to Hayne. Webster

> **"Great occasions, when nations have been in peril, have developed and brought out some of the greatest public speakers of the world."**

had no time for immediate preparation, but the occasion brought out all the reserves in this giant, and he towered so far above his opponent that Hayne looked like a pygmy in comparison.

The pen has discovered many a genius, but the process is slower and less effective than the great occasion that discovers the public speaker. Every crisis calls out ability previously undeveloped and perhaps unsuspected.

No public speaker living was ever great enough to give out the same power and force and magnetism to an empty hall, to empty seats, that he could give to an audience capable of being fired by his theme. In the presence of the audience lies a fascination, an indefinable magnetism that stimulates all the mental faculties, and acts as a tonic and vitalizer. A public speaker can say before an audience what he could not possibly have said before he went on the platform, just as we can often say to a friend in animated conversation things which we could not possibly say when alone. As when two chemicals are united, a new substance is formed from the combination which did not exist in either alone, he feels surging through his brain the combined force of his audience, which he calls inspiration, a mighty power which did not exist in his own personality.

Actors tell us that there is an indescribable inspiration which comes from the orchestra, the footlights, the audience, which it is impossible to feel, at a cold mechanical rehearsal. There is something in a great sea of expectant faces which awakens the ambition and arouses the reserve of power which can never be felt except before an audience. The power was there just the same before, but it was not aroused.

In the presence of a great public speaker, the audience is absolutely in his power. They laugh or cry as he pleases, or rise and fall at his bidding, until he releases them from the magic spell.

What is public speaking but to stir the blood of all hearers, to so arouse their emotions that they cannot control themselves a moment

> **"What is public speaking but to stir the blood of all hearers, to so arouse their emotions that they cannot control themselves a moment longer without taking the action to which they are impelled?"**

longer without taking the action to which they are impelled?

"His words are laws" may be well said of the statesman whose orations sway the world. What art is greater than that of changing the minds of men?

Wendell Phillips so played upon the emotions, so changed the convictions of Southerners who hated him, but who were curious to listen to his public speaking, that for the time being he almost persuaded them that they were in the wrong. With the ease of a master he swayed his audience. Some who hated him in the slavery days were there, and they could not resist cheering him.

When James Russell Lowell was a student, said Wetmore Story, he and Story went to Faneuil Hall to hear Webster. They meant to hoot him for his remaining in Tyler's cabinet. It would be easy, they reasoned, to get the three

> **"A good conversationalist is one who has ideas, who reads, thinks, listens, and who has therefore something to say."**

thousand people to join them. When he began, Lowell turned pale, and Story livid. His great eyes, they thought, were fixed on them. His opening words changed their scorn to admiration, and their contempt to respect.

"He gave us a glimpse into the Holy of Holies," said another student, in relating his experience in listening to a great preacher.

If You Can Talk Well

By Dr. Orison Swett Marden

A good conversationalist is one who
has ideas, who reads, thinks, listens, and
who has therefore something to say.

— SIR WALTER SCOTT

WHEN Charles W. Eliot was president
of Harvard, he said, "I recognize but one
mental acquisition as an essential part of the
education of a lady or gentleman, namely, an
accurate and refined use of the mother-tongue."

There is no other one thing which enables
us to make so good an impression, especially
upon those who do not know us thoroughly, as
the ability to converse well.

To be a good conversationalist, able to
interest people, to rivet their attention, to draw
them to you naturally, by the very superiority
of your conversational ability, is to be the pos-
sessor of a very great accomplishment, one
which is superior to all others. It not only helps

you to make a good impression upon strangers, it also helps you to make and keep friends. It opens doors and softens hearts. It makes you interesting in all sorts of company. It helps you to get on in the world. It sends you clients, patients, customers. It helps you into the best society, even though you are poor.

A man who can talk well, who has the art of putting things in an attractive way, who can

> **"But if you are an artist in conversation, everyone who comes in contact with you will see your life-picture, which you have been painting ever since you began to talk."**

interest others immediately by his power of speech, has a very great advantage over one who may know more than he, but who cannot express himself with ease or eloquence.

No matter how expert you may be in any other art or accomplishment, you cannot use your expertness always and everywhere as you can the power to converse well. If you are a musician, no matter how talented you may be, or how many years you may have spent in perfecting yourself in your specialty, or how much it may have cost you, only comparatively few people can ever hear or appreciate your music.

You may be a fine singer, and yet travel around the world without having an opportunity of showing your accomplishment, or without anyone guessing your specialty. But wherever you go and in whatever society you are, no matter what your station in life may be, you talk.

You may be a painter, you may have spent years with great masters, and yet, unless you have very marked ability so that your pictures are hung in the salons or in the great art galleries, comparatively few people will ever see them. But if you are an artist in conversation, everyone who comes in contact with you will see your life-picture, which you have been painting ever since you began to talk. Everyone knows whether you are an artist or a bungler.

In fact, you may have a great many accomplishments which people occasionally see or enjoy, and you may have a very beautiful home and a lot of property which comparatively few people ever know about; but if you are a good converser, everyone with whom you talk will feel the influence of your skill and charm.

A noted society leader, who has been very successful in the launching of *débutantes* in society, always gives this advice to her *protégés*, "Talk, talk. It does not matter much what you say, but chatter away lightly and gayly. Nothing embarrasses and bores the average man so much as a girl who has to be entertained."

The way to learn to talk is to talk. The temptation for people who are unaccustomed to soci-

> "Nothing else will indicate your fineness or coarseness of culture, your breeding or lack of it, so quickly as your conversation. It will tell your whole life's story."

ety, and who feel diffident, is to say nothing themselves and listen to what others say.

Good talkers are always sought after in society. Everybody wants to invite Mrs. So-and-So to dinners or receptions because she is such a good talker. She entertains. She may have many defects, but people enjoy her society because she can talk well.

Conversation, if used as an educator, is a tremendous power developer; but talking without thinking, without an effort to express oneself with clearness, conciseness, or efficiency, mere chattering, or gossiping, the average society small talk, will never get hold of the best thing in a man. It lies too deep for such superficial effort.

Nothing else will indicate your fineness or coarseness of culture, your breeding or lack of it, so quickly as your conversation. It will tell your whole life's story. What you say, and how you say it, will betray all your secrets, will give the world your true measure.

There is no other accomplishment or acquirement which you can use so constantly and effectively, which will give so much pleasure to your friends, as fine conversation. There is no doubt that the gift of language was intended to be a much greater accomplishment than the majority of us have ever made of it.

Most of us are bunglers in our conversation, because we do not make an art of it; we do not take the trouble or pains to learn to talk well. We do not read enough or think enough. Most of us express ourselves in sloppy, slipshod English, because it is so much easier to do so than it is to think before we speak, to make an effort to express ourselves with elegance, ease, and power.

Poor conversers excuse themselves for not trying to improve by saying that "good talkers are born, not made." We might as well say that good lawyers, good physicians, or good merchants are born, not made. None of them would ever get very far without hard work. This is the price of achievement that is of value.

> **"Many a man owes his advancement very largely to his ability to converse well."**

Many a man owes his advancement very largely to his ability to converse well. The ability to interest people in your conversation, to hold them, is a great power. The man who bungles in his expression, who knows a thing, but never can put it in logical, interesting, or commanding language, is always placed at a great disadvantage.

I know a business man who has cultivated the art of conversation to such an extent that it is a great treat to listen to him. His language flows with such liquid, limpid beauty, his words are chosen with such exquisite delicacy, taste, and accuracy, there is such a refinement in his diction that he charms everyone who hears him speak. All his life he has been a reader of the finest prose and poetry, and has cultivated conversation as a fine art.

You may think you are poor and have no chance in life. You may be situated so that others are dependent upon you, and you may not

> **"Every book you read, every person with whom you converse, who uses good English, can help you."**

be able to go to school or college, or to study music or art, as you long to; you may be tied down to an iron environment; you may be tortured with an unsatisfied, disappointed ambition: and yet you can become an interesting talker, because in every sentence you utter you can practice the best form of expression. Every book you read, every person with whom you converse, who uses good English, can help you.

Few people think very much about how they are going to express themselves. They use the first words that come to them. They do not think of forming a sentence so that it will have beauty, brevity, transparency, power. The words flow from their lips helter-skelter, with little thought of arrangement or order.

Now and then we meet a real artist in conversation, and it is such a treat and delight that we wonder why the most of us should be such bunglers in our conversation, that we should

> **"We know other people who talk very little, but whose words are so full of meat and stimulating brain force that we feel ourselves multiplied many times by the power they have injected into us."**

make such a botch of the medium of communication between human beings, when it is capable of being made the art of arts.

I have met a dozen persons in my lifetime who have given me such a glimpse of its superb possibilities that it has made all other arts seem comparatively unimportant to me.

I was once a visitor at Wendell Phillips's

home in Boston, and the music of his voice, the liquid charm of his words, the purity, the transparency of his diction, the profundity of his knowledge, the fascination of his personality, and his marvelous art of putting things, I shall never forget. He sat down on the sofa beside me and talked as he would to an old schoolmate, and it seemed to me that I had never before heard such exquisite English. I have met several English people who possessed that marvelous power of "soul in conversation which charms all who come under its spell."

Mrs. Mary A. Livermore, Julia Ward Howe, and Elizabeth Stuart Phelps Ward had this wonderful conversational charm, as has ex-President Eliot of Harvard.

The quality of the conversation is everything. We all know people who use the choicest language and express their thoughts in fluent, liquid diction, who impress us by the wonderful flow of their conversation; but that is all there is to it. They do not impress us with their thoughts; they do not stimulate us to action. We do not feel any more determined to do something in the world, to be somebody, after we have heard them talk than we felt before.

We know other people who talk very little, but whose words are so full of meat and stimulating brain force that we feel ourselves multiplied many times by the power they have injected into us.

In olden times the art of conversation reached a much higher standard than that of today. The deterioration is due to the complete revolution in the conditions of modern civiliza-

> "Good reading, however, will not only broaden the mind and give new ideas, but it will also increase one's vocabulary, and that is a great aid to conversation."

tion. Formerly people had almost no other way of communicating their thoughts than by speech. Knowledge of all kinds was disseminated almost wholly through the spoken word. There were no great daily newspapers, no magazines or periodicals of any kind.

The great discoveries of vast wealth in the precious minerals, the new world opened up by inventions and discoveries, and the great impetus to ambition have changed all this. In this lightning-express age, in these strenuous times, when everybody has the mania to attain wealth and position, we no longer have time to reflect with deliberation, and to develop our powers of conversation. In these great newspaper and periodical days, when everybody can get for a few cents the news and information which it has cost thousands of dollars to collect, everybody sits behind the morning sheet or is buried in a book or magazine. There is no longer the same need of communicating thought by the spoken word, as there was formerly.

Public speaking is becoming a lost art for the same reason. Printing has become so cheap that even the poorest homes can get more reading for a few dollars than kings and noblemen could afford in the Middle Ages. It is a rare thing to find a polished conversationalist today. So rare is it to hear one speaking exquisite English, and using a superb diction, that it is indeed a luxury.

Good reading, however, will not only broaden the mind and give new ideas, but it will also increase one's vocabulary, and that is a great aid to conversation. Many people have good thoughts and ideas, but they cannot express them because of the poverty of their vocabulary. They have not words enough to clothe their ideas and make them attractive. They talk around in a circle, repeat and repeat, because, when they want a particular word to convey their exact meaning, they cannot find it.

If you are ambitious to talk well, you must be as much as possible in the society of well-bred, cultured people. If you seclude yourself, though you are a college graduate, you will be a poor converser.

> **"Everywhere we see people placed at a tremendous disadvantage because they have never learned the art of putting their ideas into interesting, telling language."**

We all sympathize with people, especially the timid and shy, who have that awful feeling of repression and stifling of thought, when they make an effort to say something and cannot. Timid young people often suffer keenly in this way in attempting to declaim at school or college. But many a great public speaker went through the same sort of experience when he first attempted to speak in public, and was often

48

deeply humiliated by his blunders and failures. There is no other way, however, to become a public speaker or a good conversationalist than by constantly trying to express oneself efficiently and elegantly.

If you find that your ideas fly from you when you attempt to express them, that you stammer and flounder about for words which you are unable to find, you may be sure that every honest effort you make, even if you fail in your attempt, will make it all the easier for you to speak well the next time. It is remarkable, if one keeps on trying, how quickly he will conquer his awkwardness and self-consciousness, and will gain ease of manner and facility of expression.

Everywhere we see people placed at a tremendous disadvantage because they have never learned the art of putting their ideas into interesting, telling language. We see brainy men at public gatherings, when momentous questions are being discussed, sit silent, unable to tell what they know, when they are infinitely better informed than those who are making a great deal of display of public speaking or smooth talk.

People with a lot of ability, who know a great deal, often appear like a set of dummies in company, while some superficial, shallow-brained person holds the attention of those present simply because he can tell what he knows in an interesting way. They are constantly humiliated and embarrassed when away from those who happen to know their real worth, because they cannot carry on an intelligent conversation upon any topic. There are hundreds of these silent people at our national capital—many of them wives of husbands who have suddenly and unexpectedly come into political prominence.

Many people—and this is especially true of scholars—seem to think that the great *desideratum* in life is to get as much valuable information into the head as possible. But it is just as important to know how to give out knowledge in a palatable manner as to acquire it. You may be a profound scholar, you may be well read in history and in politics, you may be wonderfully well-posted in science, literature, and art, and yet, if your knowledge is locked up within you, you will always be placed at a great disadvantage.

Locked-up ability may give the individual some satisfaction, but it must be exhibited, expressed in some attractive way, before the world will appreciate it or give credit for it. It does not matter how valuable the rough diamond may be, no explaining, no describing its marvels of beauty within, and its great value, would avail; no body would appreciate it until

> **"Conversation is to the man what the cutting of the diamond is to the stone. The grinding does not add anything to the diamond. It merely reveals its wealth."**

it was ground and polished and the light let into its depths to reveal its hidden brilliancy. Conversation is to the man what the cutting of the diamond is to the stone. The grinding does not add anything to the diamond. It merely reveals its wealth.

How little parents realize the harm they are doing their children by allowing them to grow up ignorant of or indifferent to the marvelous possibilities in the art of conversation! In the majority of homes, children are allowed to mangle the English language in a most painful way.

Nothing else will develop the brain and character more than the constant effort to talk well, intelligently, interestingly, upon all sorts of topics. There is a splendid discipline in the constant effort to express one's thoughts in clear language and in an interesting manner. We know people who are such superb conversers that no one would ever dream that they have not had the advantages of the higher schools. Many a college graduate has been silenced and put to

> **"Many a college graduate has been silenced and put to shame by people who have never even been to a high school, but who have cultivated the art of self-expression."**

shame by people who have never even been to a high school, but who have cultivated the art of self-expression.

The school and the college employ the student comparatively a few hours a day for a few years; conversation is a training in a perpetual school. Many get the best part of their education in this school.

Conversation is a great ability discoverer, a great revealer of possibilities and resources. It stimulates thought wonderfully. We think more of ourselves if we can talk well, if we can interest and hold others. The power to do so increases our self-respect, our self-confidence.

No man knows what he really possesses until he makes his best effort to express to others what is in him. Then the avenues of the mind fly open, the faculties are on the alert. Every good converser has felt a power come to him from the listener which he never felt

> **"To converse well one must listen well also. This means one must hold oneself in a receptive attitude."**

before, and which often stimulates and inspires to fresh endeavor. The mingling of thought with thought, the contact of mind with mind, develops new powers, as the mixing of two chemicals produces a new third substance.

To converse well one must listen well also. This means one must hold oneself in a receptive attitude.

We are not only poor conversationalists,

but we are poor listeners as well. We are too impatient to listen. Instead of being attentive and eager to drink in the story or the information, we have not enough respect for the talker to keep quiet. We look about impatiently, perhaps snap our watch, play a tattoo with our fingers on a chair or a table, hitch about as if we were bored and were anxious to get away, and interrupt the speaker before he reaches his conclusion. In fact, we are such an impatient peo-

> **"One cause for our conversational decline is a lack of sympathy. We are too selfish, too busily engaged in our own welfare, and wrapped up in our own little world, too intent upon our own self-promotion to be interested in others."**

ple that we have no time for anything except to push ahead, to elbow our way through the crowd to get the position or the money we desire. Our life is feverish and unnatural. We have no time to develop charm of manner, or elegance of diction. "We are too intense for epigram or repartee. We lack time."

We have no time for the development of a

fine manner; the charm of the days of chivalry and leisure has almost vanished from our civilization. A new type of individual has sprung up. We work like Trojans during the day, and then rush to a theater or other place of amusement in the evening. We have no time to make our own amusement or to develop the faculty of humor and fun-making as people used to do. We pay people for doing that while we sit and laugh. We are like some college boys, who depend upon tutors to carry them through their examinations—they expect to buy their education ready-made.

Life is becoming so artificial, so forced, so diverse from naturalness, we drive our human engines at such a fearful speed, that our finer life is crushed out. Spontaneity and humor, and the possibility of a fine culture and a superb charm of personality in us are almost impossible and extremely rare.

One cause for our conversational decline is a lack of sympathy. We are too selfish, too busily engaged in our own welfare, and wrapped up in our own little world, too intent upon our own self-promotion to be interested in others. No one can make a good converser who is not sympathetic. You must be able to enter into another's life, to live it with the other person, in order to be a good talker or a good listener.

Walter Besant used to tell of a clever woman who had a great reputation as a conversationalist, though she talked very little. She had such a cordial, sympathetic manner that she helped the timid and the shy to say their best things, and made them feel at home. She dissipated their fears, and they could say things to her which they could not say to anyone else.

> "No matter how much you may know about a subject, if it does not happen to interest those to whom you are talking, your efforts will be largely lost."

People thought her an interesting conversationalist because she had this ability to call out the best in others.

If you would make yourself agreeable you must be able to enter into the life of the people with whom you converse, and you must touch them along the lines of their interest. No matter how much you may know about a subject, if it does not happen to interest those to whom you are talking, your efforts will be largely lost.

It is pitiable, sometimes, to see men standing around at the average reception or club gathering, dumb, almost helpless, and powerless to enter heartily into the conversation because they are in a subjective mood. They are thinking, thinking; thinking business, business, business; thinking how they can get on a little faster—get more business, more clients, more patients, or more readers for their books, or a better house to live in; how they can make more show. They do not enter heartily into the lives of others, or abandon themselves to the occasion enough to make good talkers. They are cold and reserved, distant, because their minds are somewhere else, their affections on themselves and their own affairs. There are only two things that interest them, business and their own little world. If you talk about these things, they are interested at once; but they do not care a snap about your affairs, how you get on, or what your ambition is, or how they can help you. Our conversation will never reach a high standard while we live in such a feverish, selfish, and unsympathetic state.

Great conversationalists have always been

very tactful—interesting without offending. It does not do to stab people if you would interest them, nor to drag out their family skeletons. Some people have the peculiar quality of touching the best that is in us; others stir up the bad. Every time they come into our presence they irritate us. Others allay all that is disagreeable. They never touch our sensitive spots, sore spots, and they call out all that is spontaneous and sweet and beautiful.

Lincoln was master of the art of making himself interesting to everybody he met. He put

> **"You must be broad, tolerant. A narrow, stingy soul never talks well."**

people at ease with his stories and jokes, and made them feel so completely at home in his presence that they opened up their mental treasures to him without reserve. Strangers were always glad to talk with him, because he was so cordial and quaint, and always gave more than he got.

A sense of humor such as Lincoln had is, of course, a great addition to one's conversational powers. But not everyone can be funny; and, if you lack the sense of humor, you will make yourself ludicrous by attempting to be so.

You must be broad, tolerant. A narrow, stingy soul never talks well. A man who is always violating your sense of taste, of justice, and of fairness, never interests you. You lock tight all the approaches to your inner self, every avenue is closed to him. Your magnetism and your helpfulness are thus cut off, and the conversation is perfunctory, mechanical, and without life or feeling.

> **"No amount of natural ability or education or good clothes, no amount of money, will make you appear well if you cannot express yourself in good language."**

You must bring your listener close to you, must open your heart wide, and exhibit a broad, free nature, and an open mind. You must be responsible, so that he will throw wide open every avenue of his nature and give you free access to his heart of hearts.

If a man is a success anywhere, it ought to be in his personality, in his power to express himself in strong, effective, interesting language. He should not be obliged to give a stranger an inventory of his possessions in order to show that he has achieved something. A greater wealth should flow from his lips, and express itself in his manner.

No amount of natural ability or education or good clothes, no amount of money, will make you appear well if you cannot express yourself in good language.

RECOMMENDED READING
The Classics

Selling Things, by Orison Swett Marden

Character: The Grandest Thing in the World, by Orison Swett Marden

The Hour of Opportunity, by Orison Swett Marden

The Miracle of Right Thought, by Orison Swett Marden

50 Lessons in 50 Years, by Garry Kinder

Speaking Secrets of the Masters, by Speakers Roundtable

Insights Into Excellence, by Speakers Roundtable

Freedom From Fear, by Mark Matteson

Focus or Failure, by James H. Amos, Jr.

Billionaire: Secrets to Success, by Bill Bartmann

The Ultimate Gift, by Jim Stovall

Positive Impact, by Charlie "T" Jones and Gregory Scott Reid

The Twelve Immutable Laws of Humor, by Billy Riggs

The Fred Factor, by Mark Sanborn

Stairway to Success, by Nido R. Quebein

There Are No Limits, by Danny Cox

Developing the Leaders Around You, by John C. Maxwell

Something For Nothing, by Brian Tracy

The Power of Positive Thinking, by Norman Vincent Peale

It Takes Less Than One Minute To Suit Up For The Lord, by Ken Blanchard

Finding Hidden Treasures, by Ron Price

The Wisdom of Andrew Carnegie, As Told To Napoleon Hill

Napoleon Hill's Magic Ladder to Success

Napoleon Hill's Keys to Positive Thinking, by Michael J. Ritt, Jr.

The Success System That Never Fails, by W. Clement Stone

Believe and Achieve, by W. Clement Stone

Your Greatest Power, by J. Martin Kohe

How To Win Friends And Influence People, by Dale Carnegie

Power of Positive Thinking, by Norman Vincent Peale

The Go-Getter, by Peter B. Kyne

I Dare You, by William Danforth

Og Mandino's University of Success

The Greatest Salesman in the World, by Og Mandino

The Richest Man in Babylon, by George S. Clason

The Secret of Success, by R.C. Allen

Acres of Diamonds, by Russell Conwell

You And Your Network, by Fred Smith

See You At The Top, by Zig Ziglar

Life Is Tremendous, by Charlie "T" Jones

Five Important Things, by Jim Paluch

Success With People, by Cavett Robert

Leadership Lessons From The Impossible Dreamer, by LuAn Mitchell-Halter

Winning Without Intimidation, by Bob Burg

The 5 Pillars of Leadership, by Paul J. Meyer

Stumbling Onto Success, by Dave Romeo

Get What You Want, by Patricia Fripp

Day By Day With James Allen, by Vic Johnson

Order *Life-Changing Classics* that have stood the test of time.

Now you can build your life or business with a collection of low cost, high content handouts! This set of extraordinary books contains titles that are life-changing yet easy to read...

Acres of Diamonds by Russell Conwell

Maxims of Life & Business by John Wanamaker

Books Are Tremendous by Charlie "Tremendous" Jones

Bradford, You're Fired! by William W. Woodbridge

That Something by William W. Woodbridge

As a Man Thinketh by James Allen

The Reason Why by R.A. Laidlaw

A Message to Garcia by Elbert Hubbard

Advantages of Poverty by Andrew Carnegie

Succeeding With What You Have by Charles Schwab

Order From:
www.ExecutiveBooks.com
1-800-233-2665